AMAZING REPTILES

Pythons

by Christine Zuchora-Walske

Content Consultant
Leonard Jones, BA
Graduate Student, Leache Lab
University of Washington

Core Library

An Imprint of Abdo Publishing
www.abdopublishing.com

www.abdopublishing.com

Published by Abdo Publishing, a division of ABDO, PO Box 398166, Minneapolis, Minnesota 55439. Copyright © 2015 by Abdo Consulting Group, Inc. International copyrights reserved in all countries. No part of this book may be reproduced in any form without written permission from the publisher. Core Library™ is a trademark and logo of Abdo Publishing.

Printed in the United States of America, North Mankato, Minnesota
042014
092014

THIS BOOK CONTAINS
RECYCLED MATERIALS

Cover Photo: Shutterstock Images
Interior Photos: Shutterstock Images, 1, 4, 8 (top), 8 (middle top), 8 (middle bottom), 8 (bottom), 20, 34 iStockphoto/Thinkstock, 7; Nikolai Pozdeev/Shutterstock Images, 10; Lakeview Images/Shutterstock Images, 12; NHPA/SuperStock, 15, 22, 32; Carol Buchanan/F1online/Glow Images, 17; Biosphoto/SuperStock, 18; John Cancalosi/National Geographic/SuperStock, 24; Kuznetsov Alexey/Shutterstock Images, 26; Red Line Editorial, 28; Lori Oberhofer/National Park Service/AP Images, 30; Dean Pennala/Shutterstock Images, 37; Mark Boulton/Alamy, 38; Natalie Jean/Shutterstock Images, 40

Editor: Mirella Miller
Series Designer: Becky Daum

Library of Congress Control Number: 2014902278

Cataloging-in-Publication Data
Zuchora-Walske, Christine.
 Pythons / Christine Zuchora-Walske.
   p. cm. -- (Amazing reptiles)
Includes bibliographical references and index.
ISBN 978-1-62403-373-5
1. Pythons--Juvenile literature.   I. Title.
597.96/78--dc23

2014902278

CONTENTS

CHAPTER ONE

Splendid Snakes

An amethystine python slithers along a tree branch in the Indonesian rain forest. It loops and curls its long, brown body around the branch. Then it sits perfectly still and becomes invisible. The snake blends into the tree bark.

A big, white cockatoo swoops in. It lands several feet away from the python on the same branch. The python does not move. The bird shuffles along the

The amethystine python is the largest snake species to live in Australia.

Amethystine Python

The amethystine python is one of the biggest pythons. It can grow up to 16 feet (5 m) long. It is a slim python for its length. It is a dull, olive brown or greenish-yellow color in the shade. But its scales shimmer purplish-blue (like the gemstone amethyst) in the sun.

branch, nibbling noisily on seeds. It is inching toward the python. But the cockatoo is too busy eating to notice the snake.

The python strikes. It grabs the bird with its long, grooved teeth, hanging onto the branch with its body. It quickly coils around the struggling cockatoo. The snake tightens until the bird cannot breathe. A few minutes later, the bird stops struggling. It is dead. Now it is mealtime for the python. It opens its mouth wide and swallows the cockatoo whole. Soon the bird is nothing but a big bulge in the python's skinny body.

Snakes of All Sizes

The amethystine python is one of 40 python species. These snakes range in size from miniature

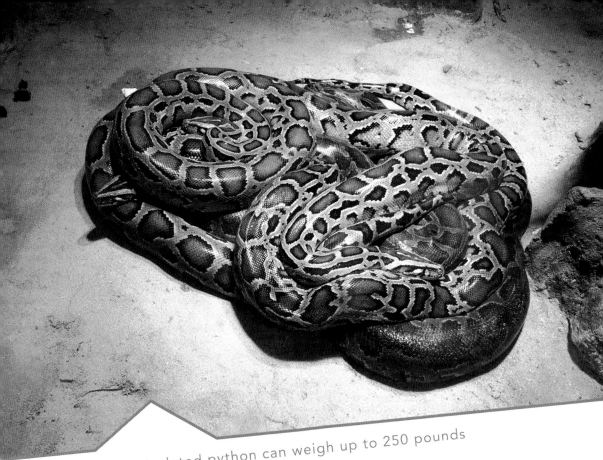

A reticulated python can weigh up to 250 pounds (113 kg).

to monstrous. Pythons are famous for their ability to grow very large. The reticulated python is the world's longest snake. It can grow up to 33 feet (10 m) long.

But not all pythons are that big. The pygmy python is the smallest member of the python family. It is only approximately 23 inches (58 cm) long and weighs approximately 7 ounces (198 g) when fully grown.

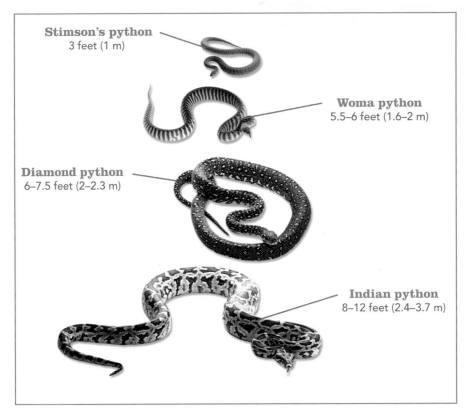

Stimson's python
3 feet (1 m)

Woma python
5.5–6 feet (1.6–2 m)

Diamond python
6–7.5 feet (2–2.3 m)

Indian python
8–12 feet (2.4–3.7 m)

Sizing Up the Snakes

This chart shows the typical sizes of a few well-known python species. Are their size differences larger or smaller than you imagined after reading about python sizes? How might the size of a python change the way it lives in the wild?

A Python's Body

Big or small, all pythons share certain physical traits.

They are members of the reptile class of animals.

That means they are cold-blooded. They rely on their

surroundings to keep their bodies warm. They also

have scaly skin. These hard scales protect pythons'
bodies from the environment and predators.

Python skins come in many different colors. A
python may be all one color. Or it may have spots,
speckles, stripes, or complex patterns. Python colors
include white, yellow, brown, red, and black.

Pythons have some body parts that other snakes
do not. They have two lungs, while most snakes have
only one lung. Pythons
also have vestigial legs.
These are tiny traces of
hind legs. These body
parts show that pythons
are more closely related
to lizards than are other
snakes. Pythons were
among the first snakes to
appear on Earth.

Granddaddy Snake

About 60 million years ago,
an ancient relative of the
python slithered around
the rain forests of South
America. Modern pythons
and their cousins can be big,
but this ancient snake was
the granddaddy of them all.
It weighed approximately
2,500 pounds (1,140 kg) and
stretched nearly 43 feet
(13 m) from its nose to the
end of its tail.

Some pythons are brightly colored, such as the green tree python.

The American Museum of Natural History held an exhibition on Charles Darwin from 2005 to 2006. This exhibit sign explains how pythons developed through the years:

> Snakes don't have legs, right? Wrong—look closely! Pythons and boa constrictors have tiny hind leg bones buried in muscles toward their tail ends. Such features, either useless or poorly suited to performing specific tasks, are described as vestigial. . . . Vestigial legs are a clue that snakes descended from lizards. Over 100 million years ago, some lizards happened to be born with smaller legs, which, in certain environments, helped them move about. . . . Over time, all members of the group were born with shorter legs, and eventually with no legs at all. Almost. The ancestor of boas and pythons retained very small vestigial legs . . .

> Source: American Museum of Natural History. "Vestigial Organs." American Museum of Natural History: Darwin Exhibition. November 2005 to August 2006. Web. Accessed November 13, 2013

Back It Up

Read this exhibit sign carefully. The author is using evidence to support a point. Write a paragraph describing the point the exhibit is making. Then write down two or three pieces of evidence the author uses to make the point.

CHAPTER TWO

The Life of a Python

Like most snakes, pythons can live for a long time. A python in the wild usually lives 20 to 25 years. Some wild pythons live as long as 35 years.

Mating

When pythons are between two and eight years old, they are ready to mate. The right time varies by species. It has more to do with size than age.

Most pythons are ready to mate when they are two-thirds to three-quarters grown.

Pythons have complex mating rituals. The female crawls around. The male follows her wherever she goes. He tries to crawl over her. The pythons flick their tongues in and out, smelling each other. Sometimes the snakes lift their heads and sway back and forth.

Nesting

A female python carrying eggs usually does not eat. Her digestive system rests during this time. She basks in the sun a lot while she is carrying the eggs. This keeps her body warm, which helps her grow healthy eggs.

Captive Pythons

Captive pythons are pythons kept as pets or in zoos. These pythons often live longer than wild pythons. Captive pythons have easier lives than their wild relatives. They have good shelter, plenty of food, and no predators. A python at the Highland Park Zoo in Pittsburgh, Pennsylvania, lived for 47 years!

Approximately one month after becoming pregnant, a mother python sheds her skin. A fresh new layer of skin lies beneath. Approximately two months after that, she lays her eggs.

A female python coils her body around her eggs to keep them warm.

The mother needs six to ten hours to lay all her eggs. Large pythons may lay more than 100 eggs. Small pythons may lay only two eggs.

Most python mothers stay with their eggs. The mother collects her eggs in a clump. She keeps them warm. She protects them from predators. She usually only leaves them if she needs water.

If the air gets too cold, large pythons can raise their body temperature a few degrees. The mother slowly squeezes and relaxes the muscles all along her body. This is a type of shivering. It looks like the python has the hiccups. As the mother's body warms up, so do her eggs.

Baby Pythons

Baby pythons develop inside their eggs for two to three months. Hatching is tiring. For the first one or two days of life, a hatchling sits inside its open shell and rests. It gets used to breathing air. It also absorbs the egg yolk through its belly.

The babies crawl out of their eggshells once they are rested. The smallest python hatchlings are approximately 10 inches (25 cm) long. The largest

Shedding

Pythons shed their outer layer of skin several times a year. Young snakes that are still growing shed more often. A python starts shedding by rubbing its head on a rough object. Rubbing loosens the skin around the head. After freeing its head, the python crawls out of the old skin.

When baby pythons are ready to hatch, they slit the leathery eggshell with their egg teeth. Then they poke their heads out.

hatchlings are approximately 27 inches (69 cm) long. Soon the mother leaves and the babies are on their own. They must hunt for food and keep safe all by themselves.

CHAPTER THREE

Patient Predators

Pythons can grow very large. Moving their bodies may take a lot of work. Pythons crawl in a way that helps them save energy. It is called rectilinear progression. This type of crawling is also called "rib-walking."

The snake uses its muscles to lift a set of its belly scales. It pushes the scales forward. This makes the ends of the scales poke out like little daggers. The

The special way pythons crawl works on the ground as well as in trees.

A python's scales help it move slowly across the ground.

snake then stabs the scale ends into the ground. Then it pushes its belly scales backward. Because the scales are stuck into the ground, the rest of the snake's body moves forward. All along the snake's body, different sets of scales do this at different times.

The python slides forward in a smooth, straight line. It is a slow way to go. Pythons can move only approximately one mile (1.6 km) per hour. But this is not all bad. Moving slowly helps pythons stay hidden.

Python Menu

Pythons will eat nearly any live prey they can catch. Depending on the size of the snake, it may eat rodents, rabbits, birds, lizards, monkeys, wallabies, pigs, and antelope. Large pythons will even eat dangerous animals such as leopards, bobcats, or alligators. They very rarely attack and eat people too.

Finding Food

Staying hidden is important for a python. Pythons are ambush hunters. They hide from their prey until it gets close enough for them to attack. Larger pythons

After striking, a python quickly coils its body around its prey.

mainly eat mammals and birds. Smaller pythons eat amphibians and reptiles.

Pythons use their sharp vision and keen sense of smell to find food. They "taste" the air with their tongues. This is actually how they smell. Pythons can also sense body heat from other animals. They do this using special pits lying between the scales along their jaws. The pits work at night or in areas thick with plants. This helps pythons find their prey even when they cannot see it.

Python Attack!

When a python senses prey nearby, it stays very still. When the prey gets close enough, a python strikes. It springs forward and grabs the prey with its sharp teeth.

A python squeezes its prey hard and steadily. Every time the prey breathes out, the python squeezes tighter. Soon the prey cannot breathe in at all. Without oxygen, it dies. The python soon feels the prey's heart stop beating. Then the snake stops squeezing. Now it is time to eat.

Jaws

A python may have anywhere from 100 to 150 teeth in its mouth. Tooth size depends on snake size. A 12-foot (4-m) snake has teeth approximately 0.5 inches (1.3 cm) long. Tree pythons have much longer teeth than ground pythons. Longer teeth are better at poking through birds' feathers.

A python's front teeth are longer than its back teeth.

Big Gulp

The python opens its mouth wide. It swallows the prey whole, usually headfirst. Muscles inside the snake's throat slowly pull the prey toward the stomach. The snake's skin is stretchy. Its bones and joints are flexible. It can also dislocate its lower jaw to open its mouth wider. These traits help the python swallow big animals. It can even swallow animals that seem too big to fit. Pythons move around less after eating. If the prey was very large or had hard parts such as hooves, horns, or quills, it can injure the python. Pythons are able to digest all of these animal parts, but it takes a lot of energy and time.

Pythons are normally active whenever their favorite prey is active. They are not strictly daytime or nighttime animals.

EXPLORE ONLINE

The focus of Chapter Three is about pythons as predators. The website at the link below also discusses the pythons' senses and other habits. As you know, every source is different. How is the information given on the website different from the information in this chapter? How is it the same? What new information can you learn from this website?

All about Pythons
www.mycorelibrary.com/pythons

CHAPTER FOUR

Where Pythons Live

Pythons live on the continents of Africa, Asia, and Australia. Pythons live south of the Sahara Desert in Africa. They do not live at the southern tip of Africa or on the island of Madagascar. Pythons live in India and in eastern and southeastern Asia. Pythons live in most of Australia. They do not live at the far southern tip of Australia or in Tasmania.

Some pythons seek shelter on tree branches.

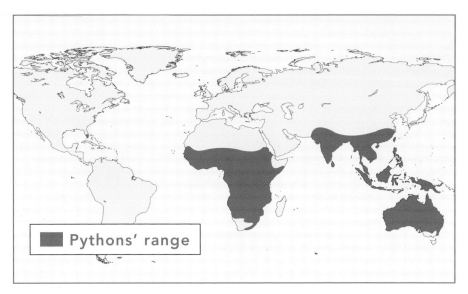

Pythons of the World

Pythons live in warm areas of Africa, Asia, Australia, and in southern Florida in the United States. This map shows where pythons make their homes. Why might pythons live in these areas? Write a few sentences describing a python's habitat.

Tasmania is a large island off Australia's southern coast.

Python Problems

Southern Florida has a large and growing population of Burmese pythons. This warm, wet part of Florida is a lot like the Burmese python's natural home. Normally it lives in the jungles and marshes of southeastern Asia. It feels at home in Florida's Everglades, a huge marshy area.

Burmese pythons are a favorite pet among snake lovers. These pythons are beautifully patterned. They grow fast. But Burmese pythons can cause problems. They grow very large. They can grow up to 23 feet (7 m) and weigh up to 200 pounds (90 kg). And sometimes Burmese pythons attack people. Some pet owners have abandoned their Burmese pythons in Florida. Others have escaped there.

Burmese pythons have no natural predators in southern Florida. They roam freely and feast on mammals and birds. Burmese pythons can lay up to 100 eggs at a time. The number of pythons in Florida has grown quickly.

Pythons in Europe

In prehistoric times, wild pythons lived in Europe. They lived in the western, southern, and eastern parts of the continent. Europe's climate was much warmer then. Europe's pythons probably died out approximately 5.2 million years ago. That is when Europe began cooling to its modern climate.

Alligators and Burmese pythons have been seen fighting in the Everglades.

Only a few lived there during the 1970s. Hundreds of thousands of Burmese pythons live there today. They are a danger to the wild animals and household pets that live there.

Warm Homes

All the places where pythons live have one thing in common. They are warm. Pythons need warm climates. Pythons are cold-blooded and rely on their surroundings to keep their bodies warm.

Different python species live in rain forests, grasslands, woodlands, swamps, rocky areas, deserts, and scrublands. Pythons live in both wet and dry places. Most can swim, and many can climb trees. Some species can do both.

Pythons may seek shelter in hollow trees, among plants or rocks, or in empty mammal

Hibernation?

Many snakes go into brumation during the winter. Brumation is when animals move and eat less. Pythons do not, however. If the temperature drops below 75 degrees Fahrenheit (24°C), they simply move less. Their digestion slows and their body temperature falls. But they cannot survive in the cold for long. They have not developed the ability to recognize fatal cold. They do not look for a warmer place to wait for the weather to change.

Some python species, such as the African rock python, burrow in rocks or in the ground.

burrows. Two Australian python species dig their own burrows. These are the woma and the black-headed python. They curve their necks and scoop dirt with their heads.

In 2012 scientists caught the largest Burmese python ever found in Florida's Everglades National Park. It was 17 feet, 7 inches (5.4 m) long. The Florida Museum of Natural History published a news story about how bad the python problem has become:

> Native to Southeast Asia and first found in the Everglades in 1979, the Burmese python is one of the deadliest and most competitive predators in South Florida. With no known natural predator, population estimates for the python range from the thousands to hundreds of thousands. They were determined to be an established species in 2000 and are a significant concern . . . . "They were here 25 years ago, but in very low numbers and it was difficult to find one because of their cryptic behavior," [herpetologist Kenneth] Krysko said. . . . "Now, you can go out to the Everglades nearly any day of the week and find a Burmese python. We've found 14 in a single day."

> Source: Danielle Torrent. "Museum Scientists Find State Record 87 Eggs in Largest Python from Everglades." Florida Museum of Natural History. August 13, 2012. Web. Accessed November 13, 2013.

What's the Big Idea?

Take a close look at this text. What is its main point about pythons in Florida? Pick out two details used to make this point. What can you tell about pythons in Florida based on this text?

CHAPTER FIVE

A Dangerous World

Pythons may seem difficult to harm. But even for pythons, the world is a dangerous place. Many animals eat small, young pythons. A wide variety of birds, wild dogs, hyenas, large frogs, large insects and spiders, and other snakes may eat baby pythons.

As young pythons grow bigger, fewer animals dare to attack them. But even adult pythons face the

A python has predators despite its size. A python is most vulnerable after it eats a big meal.

risk of being attacked. After eating, they cannot move very well. Lions, leopards, tigers, hyenas, crocodiles, and large birds of prey have been known to kill and eat pythons.

Pythons defend themselves from attacking predators. Some pythons try to escape. Some bite their attackers. Others wrap their bodies around attackers and squeeze with all their might. The ball python of Africa has a unique trick. When it senses danger, it rolls into a tight, round ball. It tucks its head deep inside the ball.

Pythons vs. People

Humans present the biggest danger to

Daring Duo

Otters are common prey for pythons. But in one case, this small mammal turned the tables on its giant reptilian predator. A naturalist wrote of finding a 17-foot (5.2-m) Indian python killed by a pair of otters. The otters had attacked the python from both sides. They avoided harm because they were so quick and nimble.

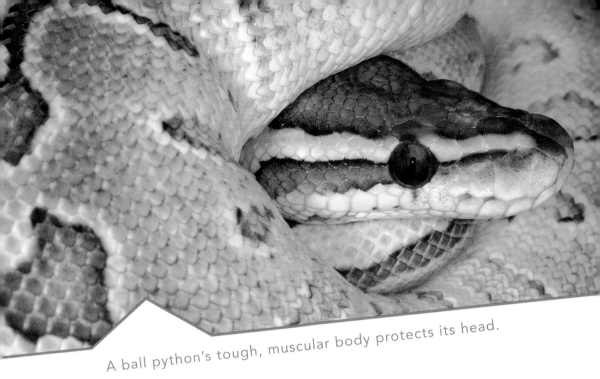

A ball python's tough, muscular body protects its head.

pythons. People kill many pythons, both accidentally and on purpose.

Pythons and people often live side by side. Pythons may live in backyards, in basements, and on roofs. Pythons may also live on or near farms or gardens. Mice, rats, rabbits, and other small mammals are plentiful in these places. Pythons eat these animals. Some people like the pest control that pythons provide. But others fear pythons or consider

People use pythons' beautiful skins for luxury leather goods, such as handbags, wallets, and shoes.

them pests. They kill pythons when they find them. They may run over pythons on roads.

People kill pythons for other reasons too. They use their skins for musical instruments. Some people also eat python meat. They may use the meat and organs in traditional medicine. Many people capture wild pythons to sell as pets. And pythons everywhere are losing their natural habitats. These problems are hurting python populations.

The International Union for Conservation of Nature (IUCN) keeps track of the most endangered animals in the world. Two python species are on the IUCN's list of at-risk animals. They are the woma python of Australia and the Burmese python of Southeast Asia.

Protecting Pythons

Conservation groups work to protect pythons from hunting and losing their natural homes. These groups raise money. They use the money to send scientists to places where pythons are dwindling or multiplying too fast. The scientists study the pythons and their surroundings. They look for ways to help pythons

Big Business

Python skins are big business. Each year half a million python skins from Southeast Asia are sold around the world. A villager in Indonesia might sell a python skin for $30. That skin may wind up as a handbag at a luxury store in Europe selling for $15,000. This trade is worth $1 billion per year.

Pythons are a vital link in the food chain, so it is important that humans protect their habitats.

survive. They also look for ways to control problem pythons.

Conservation groups also teach people about pythons. They explain why pythons are important in some parts of the world. Pythons have been around for millions of years. Their existence affects many other animal species. If one python species dies out, its prey may grow too numerous. This could upset the balance of the entire ecosystem. Pythons living where they do not belong upset nature's balance too. Conservation groups help people understand this.

Humans must find a way to protect pythons in places where they belong. We must also find a way to keep pythons out of places where they do not belong. We need to live responsibly with these reptiles. We can help them play their proper role in nature.

FURTHER EVIDENCE

Chapter Five gives information about dangers to pythons. What was one of the chapter's main points? What are some pieces of evidence in the chapter that support this point? Check out the website at the link below. Find some information on this website that supports the main point in this chapter. Write a few sentences explaining how the information from the website supports the chapter's main point.

Saving Pythons
www.mycorelibrary.com/pythons

Common Name: Python

Scientific Name: *Pythonidae*

Average Size: 2 to 33 feet (0.6 to 10 m) long, depending on the species

Average Weight: 7 ounces to 250 pounds (198 g to 113 kg), depending on the species

Color: White, yellow, brown, red, green, and black, depending on the species

Average Life Span: 20 to 25 years in the wild

Diet: Rodents, rabbits, birds, lizards, monkeys, wallabies, pigs, antelopes, leopards, bobcats, and alligators

Habitat: Warm areas in Central Africa, South and Southeast Asia, Australia, and southern Florida

Predators: Humans, lions, leopards, tigers, hyenas, crocodiles, and large birds of prey

Did You Know?

- A python can only crawl approximately one mile (1.6 km) per hour.
- Pythons do not crush their prey; they suffocate it.
- A python can eat animals much wider than its own body.
- A python may lay up to 100 eggs at a time.

STOP AND THINK

You Are There

Imagine that you are living in northeastern Australia, where amethystine pythons are common. You know they eat a lot of rodents and other pests, which is handy in this tropical part of Australia. But you are terrified that you'll find a 20-foot (6-m) snake eating your pet cat someday. Do you think the mayor of your town should try to get rid of the local pythons? What would you say to explain your argument to the mayor?

Say What?

Studying pythons can mean learning a lot of new vocabulary. Find five words in this book that you've never heard before. Use a dictionary to find out what they mean. Then write the meanings in your own words and use each word in a new sentence.

Tell the Tale

Write 200 words from the point of view of a python that was forced to leave its home when people took over its habitat. Be sure to set the scene, develop a sequence of events, and offer a conclusion.

Surprise Me

Learning about new animals can be interesting and surprising. Chapter Three of this book talks about how pythons hunt and what they eat. What two or three facts about a python's eating habits did you find most surprising? Why did you find these facts surprising?

GLOSSARY

ambush
a type of hunting in which the predator hides until the prey is close enough to attack

captive
kept by humans

cold-blooded
dependent on the environment to keep the body warm

hatchling
an animal that has just hatched

predator
an animal that kills and eats other animals

prey
an animal hunted and killed by another animal for food

rectilinear progression
a crawling method in which a snake uses its muscles and scales to pull its body forward in a straight line

species
a group of similar animals that are related closely enough to mate with one another

vestigial
left over from an animal's ancestors, such as a python's vestigial hind legs

LEARN MORE

Books

Dorcas, Michael E., and John D. Willson. *Invasive Pythons in the United States: Ecology of an Introduced Species*. Athens, GA: University of Georgia Press, 2011.

Raatma, Lucia. *Pythons*. New York: Scholastic, 2012.

Woodward, John. *Everything You Need to Know about Snakes and Other Scaly Reptiles*. New York: DK Publishing, 2014.

Websites

To learn more about Amazing Reptiles, visit **booklinks.abdopublishing.com**. These links are routinely monitored and updated to provide the most current information available.

Visit **www.mycorelibrary.com** for free additional tools for teachers and students.

INDEX

ABOUT THE AUTHOR

Christine Zuchora-Walske has been writing and editing books for children, parents, and teachers for more than 20 years. Christine lives in Minneapolis, Minnesota, with her husband and two children.